25 LAWS & RIGHTS EVERY JUVENILE MUST KNOW

Street · Station · Courtroom · Inside · After

"I had a lawyer.
I still didn't know what was happening to me."

I was 15 years old when the system took over my life.
I had people around me — and I was still lost.
This book is everything I wish someone had put in my hands
the day it all went wrong.

— Keenan Hudson

Written by Keenan Hudson

Keenan Hudson Enterprise LLC | DBA The Re-Entry Connect Solutions

www.thereentryconnect.org | www.keenanhudson.com

ISBN: 979-8-9964989-2-5

Philadelphia, Pennsylvania • EIN: 39-3134727

25 Laws & Rights Every Juvenile Must Know

First Edition — 2026

Written by Keenan Hudson

Keenan Hudson Enterprise LLC I DBA The Re-Entry Connect Solutions

---

For permissions, bulk orders, or speaking engagements, contact:

Keenan Hudson Enterprise LLC

PO Box 95, 521 Central Ave, Cheltenham, PA 19012

thereentryconnect@gmail.com

www.thereentryconnect.org | www.keenanhudson.com

thereentryconnect@gmail.com | www.thereentryconnect.org

The information in this book is provided for educational purposes only and does not constitute legal advice. Laws and procedures vary by state and jurisdiction. Always consult a licensed attorney in your state for advice specific to your situation.

Printed in the United States of America.

ISBN: 979-8-9964989-2-5

Published by Keenan Hudson Enterprise LLC | DBA The Re-Entry Connect Solutions

Philadelphia, Pennsylvania

ACKNOWLEDGMENTS & CREDITS

This book exists because of the people listed below. Their work, their sacrifice, their scholarship, and their love made these pages possible.

Author & Founder **Keenan Hudson**

Founder and Executive Director, Keenan Hudson Enterprise LLC. Re-Entry Commissioner, Mayor's Office of Black Male Engagement, City of Philadelphia. Author of 'The Unspoken Truth and Life Story,' 'The Re-Entry Connect Strategy Guide (Workbook),' 'It's Okay to Learn,' and 'My Unspoken Truth: The Youth Prevention Workbook.' Justice Reform Research Consultant, Bucknell University. Advisory Board Member, ALLIED Hub, Drexel University School of Education. Recipient of the 2024 Humanitarian Award.

Dedicated To **Every young person who entered the system without knowing their rights**

This book is for every child who sat in a courtroom, a holding cell, or a facility without knowing what they did not know. You deserved better. This book is the answer we owe you.

Legal Foundation **The United States Constitution**

The Fifth, Sixth, Eighth, and Fourteenth Amendments — the bedrock protections that belong to every person on American soil, regardless of age, income, race, or circumstance.

Landmark Cases Referenced **The Courts That Built Juvenile Rights**

In re Gault (1967) — constitutional rights in juvenile court. Miranda v. Arizona (1966) — the right to remain silent and to counsel. Miller v. Alabama (2012) — no mandatory life without parole for juveniles. Gideon v. Wainwright (1963) — the right to a free attorney. Graham v. Connor (1989) — protection against excessive force. Breed v. Jones

A LETTER TO YOU

From Keenan Hudson — Founder, The Re-Entry Connect Organization

To the Young Person Holding This Booklet,

I know where you are right now might feel like the worst place in the world. Maybe you just got picked up. Maybe you have been sitting in a cell for days and nobody has explained anything to you. Maybe you are reading this before anything has happened and something deep inside you is telling you to pay attention.

Listen to that voice. That voice saved my life.

When I was 15 years old, I walked into the Roundhouse — Philadelphia's homicide unit — and turned myself in. I had a lawyer. My whole family was there. Twenty people came to support me — uncles, aunts, grandmothers, cousins. And I still did not fully understand what was happening to me. I didn't know what the charges meant. I didn't know how the hearings worked. I didn't know the rights that belonged to me the second those handcuffs went on.

Nobody gave me this booklet. Nobody sat me down and said, 'Keenan, here is what you need to know before you say a single word.' I was 15, scared, grieving the mother I had just lost, and my entire future was being decided by strangers who all knew the rules of the game. I didn't.

That is not going to happen to you. Not if you read every single page of what I am putting in your hands right now.

These are not just laws written on paper somewhere. These are your weapons. The Constitution of the United States protects you. Pennsylvania law protects you. These protections exist whether the police tell you about them or not. Whether your lawyer explains them fully or not. Whether anyone in that courtroom looks like they care about your future or not.

Your job right now is to KNOW these rights.

I spent nearly 15 years incarcerated. I came home in 2016 and I have been fighting for people like you every single day since. I walk inside SCI Phoenix, SCI Chester, SCI Benner Township, and Philadelphia's juvenile justice facilities every week — not because I have to, but because I remember being exactly where you are. I remember the feeling of not knowing. Of being at the mercy of strangers. Of wishing someone had just told me the truth about what I was walking into.

This booklet is that truth.

You are not your worst moment. You are not what they charge you with. You are a human being with rights, with a future, and with someone in your corner who has been where you are and came out the other side.

Read every page. Understand every law. Share this with your family. I am rooting for you harder than you know.

In your corner — always,

Keenan Hudson

Keenan Hudson Enterprise LLC | DBA The Re-Entry Connect Solutions

Re-Entry Commissioner, Mayor's Office of Black Male Engagement, City of Philadelphia

Author — 'The Unspoken Truth and Life Story'

(1975) — double jeopardy in juvenile proceedings. Terry v. Ohio (1968) — protection against unreasonable searches. Estelle v. Gamble (1976) — the right to medical care while incarcerated.

For the 400+

SCI Phoenix, SCI Chester & SCI Benner Township

The men and women inside Pennsylvania's state prisons who trusted Keenan Hudson with their stories and their hope. Especially the over 400 individuals at SCI Phoenix newly eligible for resentencing following the Derek Lee ruling — many incarcerated for 20, 30, 40, or 50 years. Your resilience and dignity inspired every page of this book.

For the Young People

Philadelphia Juvenile Justice Center & Henry House Academy

Every young person Keenan Hudson has sat with, coached, mentored, and believed in inside these facilities. You are the reason this book was written.

Publisher

Keenan Hudson Enterprise LLC

Keenan Hudson Enterprise LLC, doing business as The Re-Entry Connect Solutions, Philadelphia, Pennsylvania. For-profit publishing and solutions entity. Written and published by Keenan Hudson, 2026.Providing reentry housing navigation, employment resources, financial literacy, life skills, entrepreneurial workshops, and book distribution to returning citizens and at-risk youth.

Academic Partners

Bucknell University & Drexel University

Bucknell University for recognizing lived expertise as a Justice Reform Research Consultant contributing to research on prison transfer systems in the Pennsylvania DOC. Drexel University ALLIED Hub, School of Education — a national literacy initiative — for including Keenan Hudson as an Advisory Board Member.

City of Philadelphia

Mayor's Office of Black Male Engagement

Under Mayor Cherelle Parker, for the commitment to reentry advocacy and for empowering Black youth and adults through policy and

A LETTER TO THE PARENT

From Keenan Hudson

Dear Parent, Guardian, or Loved One,

Your child needs you right now more than they have ever needed you before. And to show up for them fully, you need information.

The juvenile justice system moves fast and it is not designed to slow down and explain itself to you. From the moment your child is stopped by police through the arrest, the arraignment, the preliminary hearing, and every court date after — decisions are being made at every step. Most families have no idea what those decisions mean or what power they actually hold in this process.

I know this from the inside. When I was 15 years old and facing the most serious charges a person can face, my family packed a conference room. Twenty people who loved me deeply came to support me. My grandmother. My aunts. My uncles. Everyone who was left after my mother passed. But love alone was not enough. We trusted strangers with my future because we did not know we had the power to ask harder questions and demand better answers.

This booklet gives your family that power.

Inside these pages you will find the actual constitutional and Pennsylvania state laws that protect your child — from the moment they are stopped on the street through every stage of the legal process. You will learn what charge stacking means and what the law says about removing charges that cannot be proven. You will learn what 'certification as an adult' really means and how to fight it. You will learn what rights your child has inside a facility — to education, medical care, legal resources, religious practice, and protection from abuse.

Please do not wait until you are sitting in a courtroom to read this. The time to know your rights is before you need them.

Read this booklet yourself first — all the way through. Then sit down with your child and go through it together. If your child is already in the system, bring this to every court date, every attorney meeting, every visit. Use the glossary. Use the notes pages. Use the quick reference section.

You are not powerless in this process. You are your child's most important advocate. This booklet is your tool. Use it.

If you ever need support, guidance, or resources — write to us. We are a real organization run by real people who have lived this. We are here.

With deep respect,

Keenan Hudson

Keenan Hudson Enterprise LLC | PO Box 95, 521 Central Ave, Cheltenham, PA 19012

www.thereentryconnect.org | www.keenanhudson.com

community engagement.

The Philadelphia Reentry Coalition

For the collective work of advocates, organizers, and community members fighting every day to ensure that every person who comes home from incarceration has a real and genuine chance at a life worth living.

HOW TO USE THIS BOOKLET

This booklet follows the real order of events when a young person enters the justice system. Start at the beginning and read all the way through — even if you think some parts don't apply to you. You never know which law is the one that changes your situation.

PART 1	On the Street — Your rights when police stop, question, or search you (Laws 1–6)
PART 2	At the Station — Your rights when you are arrested and processed (Laws 7–13)
PART 3	In the Courtroom — Arraignment, preliminary hearings, and what comes next (Laws 14–19)
PART 4	While Incarcerated — Your rights inside a juvenile facility or adult prison (Laws 20–25)
SPECIAL	Charge Stacking — What it is and how to fight it
SPECIAL	Certification as an Adult — The full deep dive
SPECIAL	The Felony Murder Rule — What it means and the fight for change
SPECIAL	Expungement & Record Sealing — The path forward after the system

Each law entry includes:

WHY THIS BOOK WAS WRITTEN

The Purpose Behind Every Page

On April 26, 2004, at 15 years old, I walked into the Roundhouse — Philadelphia's homicide unit at 8th and Race Street — and turned myself in. My grandmother had a Bible in her hand. Twenty members of my family filled a conference room to support me. I had a lawyer. I had people who loved me. And I still had no idea what was happening to me.

I did not know what the charges against me actually meant. I did not know what a preliminary hearing was or what I was giving up when my lawyer advised me to waive it. I did not know the difference between charges running consecutively versus concurrently. I did not know that the list of six charges filed against me did not mean I was guilty of six crimes — it meant the prosecution was applying maximum pressure to get me to plead. I did not know any of the laws that were supposed to protect me.

I spent nearly 15 years in the Pennsylvania state prison system. During those years I educated myself — earned certifications, studied law, found God, and found purpose. I committed myself to understanding the system that had taken my freedom, so that when I came home, I could help others navigate it.

I came home in 2016.

• THE LAW — The actual constitutional provision or legal citation

• WHAT IT MEANS — Plain English, 7th grade level

• THE SCENARIO — A real-life story with Marcus, Jaylen, or Bianca showing the law in action

• WHAT NOT TO DO — The most common mistakes that hurt young people

• FOR PARENTS — Specific action steps for the family

• KNOW THIS — Critical insider knowledge

■ STATE LAW NOTE	This booklet focuses on federal constitutional law and Pennsylvania state law. If you are outside Pennsylvania, the constitutional rights are the same nationwide, but specific procedures and timelines may differ. Always consult a licensed attorney in your state.

Since then I have built businesses, purchased property, written books, earned a humanitarian award, and been appointed as a Re-Entry Commissioner for the City of Philadelphia. I walk inside SCI Phoenix, SCI Chester, and SCI Benner Township every single week — not because anyone requires it, but because I remember what it felt like to be inside without anyone who truly understood what I was going through.

Over 400 individuals at SCI Phoenix alone are among those affected by the second-degree murder ruling connected to Commonwealth v. Derek Lee — many incarcerated for 20, 30, 40, or even 50 years. I sit with them. I help them prepare to come home. And every single one tells me the same thing: nobody ever explained any of this to me.

That is why this book exists.

Not to replace a lawyer. Not to provide legal advice. But to do the one thing nobody did for me when I needed it most: tell the truth, in plain language, about what the law actually says and what every young person and every family has the right to know before they walk into a courtroom, a holding cell, or a facility and have their future decided by strangers.

The constitutional rights in this book belong to every young person in America. Black, white, brown. Urban, rural, suburban. Rich, poor, or in between. These rights exist whether or not anyone tells you about them.

But rights you do not know are rights you cannot use.

That is the gap this book closes.

I have watched young people plead guilty to charges that should have been dismissed. I have watched families trust systems

PART 1: ON THE STREET

Laws 1–6 • What happens when police stop or approach you

Marcus is 16. He's walking home when a police car rolls up. He doesn't know if he has to stop. He doesn't know if he has to talk. Most kids make decisions in those first 30 seconds that follow them for years. Here is what Marcus — and YOU — need to know.

LAW #1

The Right to Remain Silent

5th Amendment, U.S. Constitution | Miranda v. Arizona, 384 U.S. 436 (1966)

You do not have to answer questions from police. Period. This right exists from the very first second an officer speaks to you. Say: 'I am exercising my right to remain silent.' That is a complete sentence. That ends the conversation. Anything you say — even things that seem harmless — can be taken out of context and used against you in court. Professional investigators are trained to get you talking. Your silence is your strongest defense.

they did not understand. I have watched brilliant young minds lose years — sometimes decades — because nobody put the right information in their hands at the right time.

Not anymore.

This book is the weapon I wish I had at 15. It is the tool I wish my family had sitting in that conference room surrounded by love but completely without information.

Know your rights. Use your rights. Share this book with everyone you know.

And if you are inside a facility reading this right now — I see you. I have been exactly where you are. And I am telling you: this is not the end of your story.

Keenan Hudson

Founder & Executive Director, Keenan Hudson Enterprise LLC
Philadelphia, Pennsylvania | 2026

SCENARIO — Marcus, Age 16

An officer rolls up and asks, 'Hey, where are you coming from? I've been seeing a lot of activity around here.' Marcus feels pressure and starts explaining — where he was, who he was with, what they were doing. He thinks being cooperative will help.

What happened: Nothing Marcus said was incriminating on its own. But the names and location he gave connected him to a group already under investigation. A routine conversation became evidence. Marcus had done nothing wrong and still hurt his situation by talking.

■ REMEMBER THIS: You NEVER have to answer questions. 'I am exercising my right to remain silent' is a complete sentence. Use it.

■ WHAT NOT TO DO

• Don't explain yourself to police on the street — even if you are completely innocent

• Don't name other people, places, or times — any detail can be used

• Don't think being friendly will help you — in most cases it does not

■ FOR PARENTS — What to do right now:

Teach your child this phrase until it is automatic: 'I am exercising my right to remain silent.' Practice it out loud together. Make it a reflex, not a decision they have to make under pressure.

LAW #2

The Right to Be Free from Unreasonable Searches

TABLE OF CONTENTS

FRONT MATTER

Copyright Page

Acknowledgments & Credits

Why This Book Was Written

A Letter to You

A Letter to the Parent

How to Use This Book

PART ONE — ON THE STREET

Chapter 1 — The Right to Remain Silent

Chapter 2 — The Right Against Unreasonable Searches

Chapter 3 — The Right to Know If You Are Being Detained

Chapter 4 — The Right Against Excessive Force

Chapter 5 — Juveniles' Right to Have a Parent Present

Chapter 6 — Identification Laws — When You Must Give Your Name

PART TWO — AT THE STATION

Chapter 7 — The Right to Be Told Why You Were Arrested

Chapter 8 — The Right to an Attorney — Including a Free One

Chapter 9 — Miranda Rights — They Must Be Read to You

Chapter 10 — The Right to a Phone Call

Chapter 11 — The Right to Be Processed as a Juvenile

Chapter 12 — What Being Certified as an Adult Really Means

Chapter 13 — The Right to Be Held Separately from Adults

4th Amendment, U.S. Constitution | Terry v. Ohio, 392 U.S. 1 (1968) | 42 Pa. C.S. § 8953

Police cannot search your body, pockets, or belongings without a real reason. If an officer asks 'Can I search you?' — that question is them telling you they don't have enough to search without your permission. Say: 'I do not consent to this search.' Say it calmly. Comply physically but make your lack of consent clear. If they search anyway without a legal reason, your lawyer can challenge it and any evidence found may be thrown out of court.

SCENARIO — Marcus, Age 16

The officer asks, 'You mind if I check your bag real quick? Nothing to worry about if you're clean.' Marcus doesn't want to look like he's hiding something so he says 'Go ahead.'

What happened: By saying yes, Marcus gave up his 4th Amendment protection. His lawyer had no grounds to challenge the search or anything found inside.

■ REMEMBER THIS: When they ask to search, they don't have enough to do it without your permission. 'I do not consent to this search' is your constitutional right.

■ WHAT NOT TO DO

- **Don't say 'go ahead' or 'I don't care' — that is consent and cannot be taken back**
- **Don't physically resist — comply physically but state your non-consent verbally and clearly**

PART THREE — IN THE COURTROOM

Chapter 14 — The Right to a Prompt Hearing

Chapter 15 — The Right to Know Every Charge Against You

Chapter 16 — The Right to Bail or Release

Chapter 17 — The Right Against Double Jeopardy

Chapter 18 — The Right to Confront Witnesses

Chapter 19 — The Right Not to Testify Against Yourself

PART FOUR — WHILE INCARCERATED

Chapter 20 — The Right Against Cruel & Unusual Punishment

Chapter 21 — The Right to Education

Chapter 22 — The Right to Medical & Mental Health Care

Chapter 23 — The Right to Practice Your Religion

Chapter 24 — The Right to Access the Law Library

Chapter 25 — The Right to File Grievances Without Retaliation

SPECIAL SECTIONS

Charge Stacking — What It Is and How to Fight It

Certification as an Adult — The Full Story

The Felony Murder Rule — The Fight for Change

Expungement & Record Sealing — The Path Forward

RESOURCES & REFERENCE

Quick Reference — The Exact Words to Use

Pennsylvania Legal Resources

National Organizations

State-by-State Directory

Glossary — 40+ Words You Need to Know

■ FOR PARENTS — What to do right now:

Teach your child word for word: 'I do not consent to this search.' Physical compliance is okay. Verbal non-consent is the legal protection.

LAW #3

The Right to Know If You Are Being Detained

4th Amendment, U.S. Constitution / Florida v. Bostick, 501 U.S. 429 (1991)

Ask the officer: 'Am I being detained, or am I free to go?' If they say free to go — walk away calmly, do not run. If they say detained, you must stay but still do not have to answer questions. This one question can change everything. Most young people stand there answering questions for 10 minutes when they could have walked away after 90 seconds.

SCENARIO — Marcus, Age 16

The officer has been asking Marcus questions for 12 minutes. Marcus doesn't know if he can leave. He keeps answering, hoping the conversation will end.

What happened: Marcus was legally free to go after two minutes. The officer never had grounds to detain him. Marcus gave up 10 extra minutes of conversation because he didn't know he could leave.

■ REMEMBER THIS: Ask clearly and calmly: 'Am I being detained or am I free to go?' Then act on the answer. If free — walk, don't run.

■ WHAT NOT TO DO

- **Don't assume you must stay just because an officer is talking to you**
- **Don't run when told you are free to go — walk away calmly**

LAW #4

The Right to Be Free from Excessive Force

4th Amendment, U.S. Constitution | Graham v. Connor, 490 U.S. 386 (1989) | 18 Pa. C.S. § 508

Police can use force when necessary but NOT excessive force. If an officer strikes or slams you when you are not resisting, that is a constitutional violation. The rule is critical: Do NOT physically fight back. Resisting adds charges — assault on an officer — and makes everything worse. Comply physically, say 'I am not resisting,' then document every injury the moment you can. Report it to your family and lawyer. The fight happens in court, not on the street.

SCENARIO — Jaylen, Age 15

Jaylen was cooperative with his hands up. The officer grabbed him, spun him, and slammed him hard into a brick wall. Jaylen's instinct was to push back.

What happened: Jaylen did not push back. He said clearly, 'I am not resisting.' At the station, his injuries were photographed. His lawyer filed a motion citing excessive force, which became critical to challenging the entire encounter.

■ REMEMBER THIS: Do NOT fight back. Comply, document injuries immediately, tell your family, and let your lawyer fight it the right way — in court.

Notes Pages

A Final Word

■ **WHAT NOT TO DO**

- **Don't physically fight back — even when force is clearly wrong**
- **Don't fail to document injuries — photograph everything as soon as you are able**

■ **FOR PARENTS — What to do right now:**

If your child reports being physically mistreated, document everything immediately: photograph injuries, write down exactly what happened, badge number if known, time and location.

LAW #5

Juveniles Have the Right to Have a Parent Present During Questioning

In re Gault, 387 U.S. 1 (1967) | 42 Pa. C.S. § 6337 | Pennsylvania Juvenile Act

Before police can legally question a juvenile, they must make a reasonable effort to notify your parent or guardian. You have the right to have a parent or lawyer present before any questioning begins. Say: 'I want my parent and I want a lawyer before I answer any questions.' Then stop talking completely. Nothing that comes out of your mouth after that sentence should be about your case.

PART ONE: ON THE STREET

CHAPTER 1

LAW 1

THE RIGHT TO REMAIN SILENT

5th Amendment, U.S. Constitution | Miranda v. Arizona, 384 U.S. 436 (1966)

SCENARIO — Bianca, Age 14

An officer said in a gentle voice, 'Look, honey, I can tell you're not a bad kid. If you just tell me what happened tonight I can help make sure they go easy on you.' Bianca wanted it to be over.

What happened: Bianca started talking. Her parents were not notified until after she had given a full recorded statement. Her statement was used as the primary evidence against her.

■ REMEMBER THIS: No matter how kind they sound, no matter what they promise — say: 'I want my parent and I want a lawyer.' Then say nothing else about your case.

■ WHAT NOT TO DO

- **Don't be fooled by a friendly tone — it is an interrogation technique**
- **Don't believe promises of leniency from officers — only prosecutors can make deals**

■ FOR PARENTS — What to do right now:

If police contact you because your child is being questioned, get there immediately. If you cannot, tell them by phone: 'My child is not to be questioned until I am present and until they have an attorney.' Say it clearly.

LAW #6

Identification Laws — When You Must Give Your Name

Pennsylvania — Commonwealth v. Preacher, 827 A.2d 1235 (Pa. Super. 2003) | 18 Pa. C.S. § 5101

Pennsylvania does not require you to show ID on the street in a consensual encounter. However, if you are lawfully detained,

PART ONE: ON THE STREET

CHAPTER 2

LAW 2

THE RIGHT AGAINST UNREASONABLE SEARCHES

4th Amendment, U.S. Constitution | Terry v. Ohio, 392 U.S. 1 (1968)

you may be required to provide your name. Refusing to give your name when lawfully detained can result in an obstruction charge. Give your name if and only if you are lawfully detained. You do not have to provide your ID card, address, where you are going, or anything else. Name only. Everything else waits for a lawyer.

SCENARIO — Marcus, Age 16

Marcus was lawfully detained. The officer asked for his name and ID. Marcus had heard 'never talk to police' and refused to say absolutely anything — including his name.

What happened: Marcus was charged with obstruction for refusing to identify himself during a lawful detention. It added an extra charge to a situation that did not need one.

■ REMEMBER THIS: Name only when lawfully detained. Everything else — silent until a lawyer is present.

■ WHAT NOT TO DO

- **Don't refuse to give your name if you are lawfully detained — that creates a new charge**
- **Don't give your address, phone number, or ID beyond what is legally required**

PART ONE: ON THE STREET

CHAPTER 3

LAW 3

THE RIGHT TO KNOW IF YOU ARE BEING DETAINED

4th Amendment, U.S. Constitution | Florida v. Bostick, 501 U.S. 429 (1991)

PART 2: AT THE STATION

Laws 7–13 • From arrest through processing

Jaylen is 15. The handcuffs are on. He's in the back of a patrol car. His heart is pounding. He has never been arrested before. He does not know what is about to happen. Everything in this section is what Jaylen needed to know before that car door opened.

LAW #7

The Right to Be Told Why You Were Arrested

4th Amendment, U.S. Constitution | 42 Pa. C.S. § 6325 | Gerstein v. Pugh, 420 U.S. 103 (1975)

When you are arrested, police must have probable cause — a real, specific reason to believe you committed a crime. They are required to inform you of the reason for your arrest. You are not required to confirm, deny, or add anything. If nobody tells you why, ask your lawyer immediately. At your first court appearance, your lawyer must receive the probable cause documentation. If the probable cause is weak or false, your lawyer can challenge the legality of the entire arrest.

PART ONE: ON THE STREET

CHAPTER 4

LAW 4

THE RIGHT AGAINST EXCESSIVE FORCE

4th Amendment, U.S. Constitution | Graham v. Connor, 490 U.S. 386 (1989)

SCENARIO — Jaylen, Age 15

Jaylen was arrested but nobody told him what for. He panicked and kept explaining his version of events to every officer he saw, trying to clear himself.

What happened: Each time Jaylen spoke about his case without a lawyer present, he gave prosecutors new material. His lawyer later found the probable cause statement was thin — but Jaylen had filled in gaps they did not originally have.

■ REMEMBER THIS: You have a right to know your charges. But you find that out through your lawyer — not by talking to officers.

■ WHAT NOT TO DO

- **Don't try to explain or defend yourself before knowing the exact charges**
- **Don't fill in gaps in the officers' knowledge — let their weak case stay weak**

■ FOR PARENTS — What to do right now:

In your first conversation with your child's attorney, ask for the probable cause statement. If it is thin or incomplete, that is your first weapon.

LAW #8

The Right to an Attorney — Including a Free One

6th Amendment, U.S. Constitution | Gideon v. Wainwright, 372 U.S. 335 (1963) | In re Gault, 387 U.S. 1 (1967) | 42 Pa. C.S. § 6337

This may be the most important right in this entire booklet. You have an absolute right to a lawyer. If your family cannot afford

CHAPTER 5

LAW 5

JUVENILES' RIGHT TO HAVE A PARENT PRESENT

In re Gault, 387 U.S. 1 (1967) | 42 Pa. C.S. § 6337

one, the government is constitutionally required to provide one for free. This right applies to juveniles in delinquency proceedings just as it does to adults. Say: 'I want a lawyer. I am not answering any questions without a lawyer present.' Once you say those words, all questioning must stop by law. Your lawyer is not just someone who talks in court — they are your shield from the moment of arrest forward.

SCENARIO — Jaylen, Age 15

The investigator said calmly: 'I'm not here to railroad you. I just want to hear your side. The other guys already told us what happened. Right now you have a chance to help yourself — but that window closes fast.'

What happened: Jaylen said clearly: 'I want a lawyer. I am not answering any questions.' The investigator tried once more. Jaylen said it again. The investigator left. That decision protected Jaylen from that moment forward.

■ REMEMBER THIS: Say: 'I want a lawyer. I am not answering any questions.' Say it twice if you have to. Then stop talking completely.

■ WHAT NOT TO DO

- **Don't waive your right to a lawyer because you feel like you have nothing to hide**
- **Don't answer 'just background questions' — there are no innocent questions in an interrogation**
- **Don't think invoking your right to a lawyer makes you look guilty — it makes you smart**

CHAPTER 6

LAW 6

IDENTIFICATION LAWS — WHEN YOU MUST GIVE YOUR NAME

Commonwealth v. Preacher, 827 A.2d 1235 (Pa. Super. 2003)

■ FOR PARENTS — What to do right now:

Call the Defender Association of Philadelphia Juvenile Unit: (215) 568-3190. If outside Philadelphia, contact your county's Public Defender office the same day as the arrest.

LAW #9

Miranda Rights — They Must Be Read to You

5th & 6th Amendments | Miranda v. Arizona, 384 U.S. 436 (1966) | Berkemer v. McCarty, 468 U.S. 420 (1984)

Before police can legally question you while you are in custody, they must read you your Miranda rights: You have the right to remain silent. Anything you say can and will be used against you. You have the right to an attorney. If you cannot afford an attorney, one will be appointed. If police question you in custody WITHOUT reading these rights first, anything you say may be suppressed — thrown out of court completely. This is called a Miranda violation. If your rights were not read before questioning, tell your lawyer those exact words immediately.

SCENARIO — Bianca, Age 14

Bianca was put in a small room and an officer immediately started asking questions. No Miranda warning was given. Bianca answered for 20 minutes before an attorney arrived.

What happened: Bianca's lawyer filed a motion to suppress every statement she made before the Miranda warning. The judge agreed — all 20 minutes of statements were thrown out. The case against Bianca became significantly weaker.

■ REMEMBER THIS: If nobody read you your rights before questioning you in custody, tell your lawyer immediately. That is a violation that can erase everything you said.

■ **WHAT NOT TO DO**

- **Don't assume Miranda rights were read just because you've heard them on TV**
- **Don't waive your Miranda rights — if asked to sign a waiver, say 'I want a lawyer first'**

■ **FOR PARENTS — What to do right now:**

Ask your child: 'Were you read your Miranda rights before they asked you questions?' If the answer is no or unclear, tell the lawyer immediately. This can be one of the most powerful tools in your case.

LAW #10

The Right to a Phone Call

Standard Police Procedure | Commonwealth v. Hammond, 308 Pa. Super. 139

After processing, you have the right to make a phone call. Use it with extreme discipline. Call a parent or guardian — never a friend. Never discuss the facts of your case. Every call made from a police station or jail is recorded and can be played in court. Use the call only to communicate two things: where you are, and that you need a lawyer. That is the entire call. Nothing else.

PART TWO: AT THE STATION

CHAPTER 7

LAW 7

THE RIGHT TO BE TOLD WHY YOU WERE ARRESTED

4th Amendment, U.S. Constitution | Gerstein v. Pugh, 420 U.S. 103 (1975)

SCENARIO — Jaylen, Age 15

Jaylen called his cousin Damon and started telling him everything — 'They're saying I was there, and I was, but I didn't do nothing, I was just with Marcus and them, we were outside at like 9...'

What happened: The call was recorded. At Jaylen's hearing, the prosecutor played the exact portion where Jaylen placed himself at the scene and named Marcus. Information Jaylen gave voluntarily became evidence in court.

■ REMEMBER THIS: Phone call script: 'I've been arrested. I'm at [location]. I need a lawyer. Come as soon as you can.' That is the entire call.

■ WHAT NOT TO DO

- **Don't discuss any facts of your case on a jail or station phone — it is always recorded**
- **Don't call friends — call family or a legal guardian only**

■ FOR PARENTS — What to do right now:

When your child calls, stay calm. Get the location, confirm you will contact an attorney, and end the call. Say: 'Don't say anything else. I'm getting you a lawyer right now.' Do not ask what happened on a recorded line.

LAW #11

The Right to Be Processed as a Juvenile — Not an Adult

42 Pa. C.S. § 6302 / Pennsylvania Juvenile Act / Kent v. United States, 383 U.S. 541 (1966)

If you are under 18, you are entitled to be processed through the juvenile justice system unless the prosecution successfully

CHAPTER 8

LAW 8

THE RIGHT TO AN ATTORNEY — INCLUDING A FREE ONE

6th Amendment | Gideon v. Wainwright, 372 U.S. 335 (1963) | In re Gault, 387 U.S. 1 (1967)

certifies you as an adult. In juvenile court, proceedings are called 'adjudications,' findings are 'delinquent' not 'guilty,' and most importantly — your records can be sealed when you turn 18, giving you a real fresh start. In adult court, you face a permanent public record that shows up on every background check for the rest of your life. Fight with everything you have to stay in the juvenile system.

SCENARIO — Marcus, Age 16

Marcus was 16 and charged with aggravated assault. No one told his mother the prosecutor had already filed to certify Marcus as an adult. She assumed at 16 he would automatically be in juvenile court.

What happened: By the time the family understood what was happening, the certification hearing was three days away. They had very little time to prepare. Marcus was certified and tried as an adult. At 16, he received a permanent adult conviction that followed him for years.

■ REMEMBER THIS: The word CERTIFICATION is one of the most important words in this booklet. Ask about it from day one. Fight it from day one.

■ WHAT NOT TO DO

- **Don't assume juvenile court is automatic — certification can happen quickly and quietly**
- **Don't wait to ask your lawyer about certification risk — ask in the very first conversation**

CHAPTER 9

LAW 9

MIRANDA RIGHTS — THEY MUST BE READ TO YOU

5th & 6th Amendments | Miranda v. Arizona, 384 U.S. 436 (1966)

■ FOR PARENTS — What to do right now:

In your first conversation with the attorney, ask: 'Is the prosecution seeking to certify my child as an adult?' If yes or maybe, demand an immediate meeting on certification hearing strategy.

LAW #12

What Being Certified as an Adult Really Means

42 Pa. C.S. § 6355 | Pennsylvania Juvenile Act | Breed v. Jones, 421 U.S. 519 (1975)

Certification is the legal transfer of a juvenile's case from juvenile court to adult criminal court. A judge must hold a certification hearing and weigh multiple factors: your age, maturity, prior record, the seriousness of the offense, whether the juvenile system can rehabilitate you, community ties, and family support. This is NOT a conviction hearing — it is specifically about which system handles you. Your lawyer can and must present evidence: character witnesses, school records, mental health evaluations, community involvement. The certification fight can literally determine the entire direction of your life.

PART TWO: AT THE STATION

CHAPTER 10

LAW 10

THE RIGHT TO A PHONE CALL

Standard Police Procedure | Commonwealth v. Hammond, 308 Pa. Super. 139

SCENARIO — Marcus, Age 16

At Marcus's certification hearing, his attorney brought his teachers, football coach, and a mental health expert. He presented Marcus's clean record and community involvement. The prosecutor argued the offense was too serious for juvenile court.

What happened: The judge ruled to keep Marcus in juvenile court. The same charge that would have been a permanent adult felony became a sealed juvenile record at 18. Marcus went to college at 20. The certification fight saved his future.

■ REMEMBER THIS: The certification hearing is one of the most important moments in a juvenile's case. Prepare for it like it is the most important day of your life — because it might be.

■ WHAT NOT TO DO

- **Don't treat the certification hearing as routine — it determines everything**
- **Don't fail to gather character witnesses, school records, and community support**

■ FOR PARENTS — What to do right now:

Gather every positive document about your child immediately: school records, awards, community involvement, letters from teachers and mentors. Build the case that your child deserves to stay in the juvenile system.

LAW #13

The Right to Be Held Separately from Adults

Juvenile Justice and Delinquency Prevention Act (JJDPA) | 42 U.S.C. § 5633 | 42 Pa. C.S. § 6327

CHAPTER 11

LAW 11

THE RIGHT TO BE PROCESSED AS A JUVENILE

42 Pa. C.S. § 6302 | Kent v. United States, 383 U.S. 541 (1966)

Federal law requires juveniles in detention to be separated from adult inmates — sight and sound separation. Placing a juvenile where they can see or hear adult inmates violates federal law. Being placed in an overcrowded cell beyond its rated capacity is a violation of the 8th Amendment's protection against cruel and unusual punishment — something Keenan Hudson experienced at 15 and documented in his book. If your child is in contact with adult inmates or in an overcrowded cell, this must be raised with a lawyer immediately.

SCENARIO — Bianca, Age 14

Bianca, 14, was regularly in the same common areas as adult women awaiting trial. Two adults had repeatedly threatened her.

What happened: Bianca's mother reported this to the lawyer. An emergency motion was filed citing the JJDPA sight and sound separation requirement. The facility was given 24 hours to remedy the situation or face a federal compliance review. Bianca was moved within hours.

■ REMEMBER THIS: Federal law mandates sight and sound separation of juveniles from adults. If violated, your lawyer can seek immediate emergency relief.

■ WHAT NOT TO DO

- **Don't accept unsafe housing as 'just how it is' — violations are legally actionable**
- **Don't wait to report unsafe conditions — document and report immediately**

PART TWO: AT THE STATION

CHAPTER 12

LAW 12

WHAT BEING CERTIFIED AS AN ADULT REALLY MEANS

42 Pa. C.S. § 6355 / Breed v. Jones, 421 U.S. 519 (1975)

■ FOR PARENTS — What to do right now:

At every visit ask your child specifically about housing conditions. Are they near adults? Have they felt threatened? Document what they tell you with dates and report to the lawyer.

PART 3: IN THE COURTROOM

Laws 14–19 • Arraignment, hearings, and your day in court

The courtroom is designed to feel overwhelming. People speak in legal language that seems designed to confuse. This section is the decoder. Read it carefully and the courtroom will never feel the same way again.

ARRAIGNMENT EXPLAINED	Your FIRST appearance before a judge after arrest. The judge reads the charges out loud. You are asked to plead: Guilty, Not Guilty, or No Contest. In virtually every case your lawyer will advise NOT GUILTY at arraignment. This is standard — it preserves your right to fight. Bail conditions are also set here. Arraignment usually happens within 72 hours of arrest.

PART TWO: AT THE STATION

CHAPTER 13

LAW 13

THE RIGHT TO BE HELD SEPARATELY FROM ADULTS

JJDPA | 42 U.S.C. § 5633 | 42 Pa. C.S. § 6327

PRELIMINARY HEARING EXPLAINED	A hearing where a judge decides if there is ENOUGH EVIDENCE to send your case forward to trial. Your lawyer can cross-examine witnesses and challenge evidence here. This is NOT your trial. But it is critically important — your first real chance to see and challenge the prosecution's case. Keenan Hudson was advised to WAIVE his preliminary hearing. In his book he notes this had lasting consequences. NEVER waive the preliminary hearing without fully understanding what you are giving up.

LAW #14

The Right to a Prompt Hearing

6th Amendment, U.S. Constitution | 42 Pa. C.S. § 6335 | Pa. R. Crim. P. 540

After arrest, you have the right to appear before a judge within a reasonable and prompt time — generally within 72 hours in Pennsylvania. You cannot be held indefinitely without a court appearance. If you are held beyond that period without explanation, your lawyer can file a motion challenging the delay. Do not allow days to turn into weeks without demanding to know when your hearing is scheduled.

PART THREE: IN THE COURTROOM

CHAPTER 14

LAW 14

THE RIGHT TO A PROMPT HEARING

6th Amendment, U.S. Constitution | 42 Pa. C.S. § 6335

SCENARIO — Jaylen, Age 15

Jaylen was arrested on a Friday night and not brought before a judge until Wednesday — five full days. Nobody communicated with his family about the delay.

What happened: Jaylen's lawyer filed a motion challenging the delay. It established a pattern of procedural problems that helped frame the defense throughout the entire case.

■ REMEMBER THIS: 72 hours is the standard. If that passes without a hearing, your lawyer must file immediately.

■ WHAT NOT TO DO

- **Don't assume delays are routine — document every day and report to your lawyer**

■ FOR PARENTS — What to do right now:

Track every day from the moment of arrest. If 72 hours passes without a court appearance and no explanation, contact the lawyer immediately and ask them to file a motion.

LAW #15

The Right to Know Every Charge Against You

6th Amendment, U.S. Constitution / 42 Pa. C.S. § 6335(a) / Pennsylvania Rules of Criminal Procedure

You have the right to a written statement of every charge filed against you and to understand what each one means and what it carries as a potential penalty. Prosecutors commonly 'stack' charges — filing many separate charges from a single incident — to maximize pressure for a plea deal. You do not have to accept the stack. Each charge must be individually proven. If a

PART THREE: IN THE COURTROOM

CHAPTER 15

LAW 15

THE RIGHT TO KNOW EVERY CHARGE AGAINST YOU

6th Amendment, U.S. Constitution | 42 Pa. C.S. § 6335(a)

charge cannot be proven, it must be withdrawn or dismissed. Your lawyer's job is to fight each charge individually and demand the removal of every charge for which the prosecution lacks evidence.

SCENARIO — Marcus, Age 16

Marcus was charged with six separate offenses from a single incident. His family was overwhelmed. They urged him to just take the first plea deal to make it stop. The deal included one felony that would follow Marcus as an adult.

What happened: Marcus's lawyer filed motions challenging three of the six charges for lack of evidence. Two were dismissed before trial and one was reduced. Marcus went in facing three charges instead of six — which significantly changed the outcome.

■ REMEMBER THIS: Six charges does not mean six crimes. Every charge must be individually proven. Fight each one.

■ WHAT NOT TO DO

- **Don't be overwhelmed into a plea because the charge list looks long**
- **Don't assume all charges will stick — weak charges can and must be challenged**

■ FOR PARENTS — What to do right now:

Ask the lawyer to walk through every single charge on paper — what it means, what the evidence is, which ones they plan to challenge. If your lawyer doesn't bring this up, you bring it up.

PART THREE: IN THE COURTROOM

CHAPTER 16

LAW 16

THE RIGHT TO BAIL OR RELEASE

8th Amendment, U.S. Constitution | 42 Pa. C.S. § 6325 | Stack v. Boyle, 342 U.S. 1 (1951)

■ KNOW THIS:

CHARGE STACKING: Each charge requires its own proof. A charge with no evidence must be removed. Your lawyer files a 'motion for nolle prosequi' — it means 'do not pursue.' Know this term. Ask your lawyer about it for every single charge on the list.

LAW #16

The Right to Bail or Release — Even as a Juvenile

8th Amendment, U.S. Constitution | 42 Pa. C.S. § 6325 | Stack v. Boyle, 342 U.S. 1 (1951)

Bail must be reasonable — not set to ensure pre-trial detention. For juveniles, courts can release to a parent or guardian under supervised conditions instead of requiring cash bail. For serious charges, zero bond may be set. Even with zero bond, your lawyer can challenge your conditions of confinement. Being held before trial does not make you guilty. You are innocent until proven guilty. That applies every day you are waiting.

SCENARIO — Bianca, Age 14

Bianca was charged with a non-violent first offense. The judge set bail at $20,000. Her family had nothing near that. Bianca sat in detention for three months.

What happened: Bianca's lawyer filed a formal bail reduction motion. The judge reduced bail to $1,000. Bianca went home that week and was able to participate in her defense from the outside.

■ REMEMBER THIS: Excessive bail can be challenged. A bail reduction motion is a standard legal tool. The first number is not always the final answer.

PART THREE: IN THE COURTROOM

CHAPTER 17

LAW 17

THE RIGHT AGAINST DOUBLE JEOPARDY

5th Amendment, U.S. Constitution | Breed v. Jones, 421 U.S. 519 (1975)

■ WHAT NOT TO DO

- **Don't accept the initial bail amount as permanent**
- **Don't let your child sit in detention for months without aggressively pursuing release**

■ FOR PARENTS — What to do right now:

If you cannot afford bail, tell the lawyer immediately and ask for a bail reduction motion. Bring to the hearing: proof of stable address, employment, school enrollment, family support. Show the judge your child has somewhere safe to go.

LAW #17

The Right Against Double Jeopardy

5th Amendment, U.S. Constitution | Benton v. Maryland, 395 U.S. 784 (1969) | Breed v. Jones, 421 U.S. 519 (1975)

Once you go to trial or adjudication and are found not guilty, the government cannot try you again for the same offense. This is the constitutional protection against double jeopardy. It also applies in juvenile cases: if you have been adjudicated in juvenile court for an offense, you generally cannot then be tried for the same conduct in adult court — established in Breed v. Jones. A not-guilty finding is permanent. No new evidence, no new prosecutor, no public pressure can reopen it.

PART THREE: IN THE COURTROOM

CHAPTER 18

LAW 18

THE RIGHT TO CONFRONT WITNESSES AGAINST YOU

6th Amendment, U.S. Constitution | Crawford v. Washington, 541 U.S. 36 (2004)

SCENARIO — Jaylen, Age 15

Jaylen was found not delinquent on one count of conspiracy. Six months later, new witnesses came forward and the prosecutor's office wanted to revisit that charge.

What happened: Jaylen's lawyer immediately filed a double jeopardy motion. The court agreed without extended argument — Jaylen had already been adjudicated not delinquent on that specific charge and it was permanently closed.

■ **REMEMBER THIS: Not guilty is permanent. Nobody can reopen a closed not-guilty finding. Double jeopardy is your constitutional shield.**

LAW #18

The Right to Confront Witnesses Against You

6th Amendment, U.S. Constitution | Crawford v. Washington, 541 U.S. 36 (2004)

You have the constitutional right to face the people testifying against you and to have your lawyer cross-examine them. Every prosecution witness can be questioned about their motives, memory, prior statements, relationship to you, and any deals they received in exchange for their testimony. Co-defendants who testify against you in exchange for reduced charges are among the most common witnesses in juvenile cases. Their deals must be fully disclosed and can be aggressively challenged.

SCENARIO — Marcus, Age 16

A co-defendant agreed to testify against Marcus in exchange for a reduced charge. He told the court he clearly saw Marcus do something specific. Marcus's lawyer cross-examined him for 45 minutes.

What happened: The lawyer revealed the witness had given police a different account originally, received a significant charge reduction for testifying, and had a personal dispute with Marcus from months earlier. The judge weighed the testimony with serious skepticism.

■ REMEMBER THIS: Every witness can be questioned. Every deal they got must be disclosed. Cross-examination is your weapon — make sure your lawyer uses it.

■ WHAT NOT TO DO

- **Don't assume a co-defendant's testimony is automatically believed — it can be challenged**
- **Don't let any deal a prosecution witness received stay hidden — demand full disclosure**

■ FOR PARENTS — What to do right now:

Ask your child's lawyer: 'Who are the prosecution witnesses? Have any of them received deals for testimony? What were their original statements?' These questions are your right.

LAW #19

The Right Against Self-Incrimination in Court

5th Amendment, U.S. Constitution | Malloy v. Hogan, 378 U.S. 1 (1964) | Griffin v. California, 380 U.S. 609 (1965)

You have the absolute right not to testify at your own trial or adjudication. If you choose not to take the stand, the judge or jury is constitutionally prohibited from treating your silence as evidence of guilt. The prosecutor cannot comment on your silence. This protection extends to every stage of the proceeding. Your lawyer will advise whether testifying strengthens or weakens your case. In many situations, the best defense is presenting the weaknesses in the prosecution's case without ever putting you on the stand.

SCENARIO — Bianca, Age 14

At Bianca's hearing, her lawyer advised her strongly not to testify. Bianca was scared and felt that if she didn't speak the judge would assume the worst. She almost changed her mind.

What happened: Bianca followed her lawyer's advice and did not testify. The prosecution's case was built almost entirely on the statement Bianca had made early on — which had been partially suppressed. Without Bianca giving them new material, the prosecution could not recover. She was found not delinquent.

■ REMEMBER THIS: Not testifying is not the same as being guilty. Your silence is protected by the Constitution. Trust your lawyer's judgment.

■ WHAT NOT TO DO

- **Don't let fear drive you to testify if your lawyer advises against it**
- **Don't think silence looks guilty — constitutionally, it cannot be used that way**

PART 4: WHILE INCARCERATED

Laws 20–25 • Your rights do not stop at the facility door

The walls of a facility are not the walls of your rights. The Constitution travels with you everywhere. The moment staff tells you that you have no rights inside — that is the moment you know you need to document what is happening and get word to your lawyer.

LAW #20

The Right Against Cruel and Unusual Punishment

8th Amendment, U.S. Constitution | Estelle v. Gamble, 429 U.S. 97 (1976) | Farmer v. Brennan, 511 U.S. 825 (1994)

The 8th Amendment prohibits cruel and unusual punishment inside a facility. This means you cannot be beaten by staff, denied food or water, placed in dangerous conditions, subjected to prolonged solitary confinement, or denied necessary medical care. Being forced into an overcrowded cell beyond legal capacity is a documented 8th Amendment violation — Keenan Hudson experienced this at 15 and documented it in his memoir. Solitary confinement of juveniles for extended periods is increasingly recognized by courts as cruel and unusual punishment. Document every incident — date, time, what happened, who was involved — and get this information to your family and lawyer by any available means.

SCENARIO — Jaylen, Age 15

Jaylen was placed in solitary confinement for 21 days for a minor altercation. He was 15 with no prior record, no access to school, limited time outside his cell, and no family contact for the first week.

What happened: Jaylen got a note to his mother through a counselor. His mother contacted a legal advocacy organization. An emergency petition was filed arguing that 21-day solitary confinement of a 15-year-old constituted cruel and unusual punishment. Jaylen was moved within 48 hours.

■ REMEMBER THIS: Document every day in solitary — date, conditions, access to food and air. Get that information to your family. Fight it legally.

■ WHAT NOT TO DO

- **Don't accept abusive conditions as permanent — they are legal violations**
- **Don't fail to document — memory fades, written records do not**

■ FOR PARENTS — What to do right now:

Ask at every visit: Are you in solitary? Have you been struck by staff? Are you getting food? Are you getting time outside? Write down everything they tell you with dates.

LAW #21

The Right to Education While Incarcerated

IDEA — 20 U.S.C. § 1400 / 22 Pa. Code § 11.1 / 42 Pa. C.S. § 6352

Pennsylvania law and federal law both require that juveniles in detention continue to receive educational programming. This is a legal mandate, not optional. If you have an IEP for a learning disability, attention disorder, or other special need, that IEP must be honored and implemented inside the facility. You have the right to work toward your GED or diploma. Education changed Keenan Hudson's life inside those walls. From his very first days of incarceration, he committed himself to learning — and that commitment became the foundation of everything he built when he came home.

SCENARIO — Bianca, Age 14

Bianca had an IEP for a reading disorder. When she entered the facility she was given standard materials and her IEP was ignored.

What happened: Bianca's mother brought a copy of the IEP to the facility administrator. When nothing changed, her lawyer sent a formal written notice citing federal IDEA requirements. The facility was required to implement accommodations within 10 school days. They complied within five.

■ REMEMBER THIS: Your IEP travels with you. Your education rights never stop. If they are not being honored — put it in writing and escalate immediately.

■ WHAT NOT TO DO

- **Don't let anyone tell you your IEP doesn't apply inside a facility**
- **Don't stop pursuing your education — use every resource available**

■ FOR PARENTS — What to do right now:

Bring a copy of your child's IEP to the facility on day one. Ask to speak with the educational coordinator. Confirm in writing that the IEP will be implemented. Follow up every two weeks.

LAW #22

The Right to Medical and Mental Health Care

8th Amendment, U.S. Constitution | Estelle v. Gamble, 429 U.S. 97 (1976) | 42 Pa. C.S. § 6327

Incarcerated individuals have a constitutional right to receive necessary medical and mental health care. Deliberately ignoring serious medical needs is a constitutional violation. File a sick call request every day you need care. Keep a record of every request. If you are experiencing depression, anxiety, trauma, panic attacks, or thoughts of self-harm, you have the right to mental health support. Asking for help is not weakness. Inside those walls, it is survival and it is your right.

SCENARIO — Marcus, Age 16

Marcus had severe headaches and vision problems for three weeks. He submitted five separate sick call requests. None resulted in a medical visit. A guard told him he was 'faking it for attention.'

What happened: Marcus's mother formally raised the issue at her next visit and documented the conversation. His lawyer sent a written demand for medical evaluation. Marcus was found to have dangerously elevated blood pressure needing immediate medication. The five-week delay became the basis of a formal complaint against the facility.

■ REMEMBER THIS: Submit every sick call request in writing. Keep a mental record of date, complaint, and response. Tell your family at every visit. This is your constitutional right.

■ WHAT NOT TO DO

- **Don't accept 'you'll be fine' from non-medical staff as a substitute for actual evaluation**
- **Don't stop requesting care after one or two denials — persist and document every attempt**

■ FOR PARENTS — What to do right now:

At every visit ask: Have you needed medical attention? Did you submit a sick call? Did you receive care? If care was denied, document the dates and contact the lawyer immediately.

LAW #23

The Right to Practice Your Religion

1st Amendment, U.S. Constitution | RLUIPA — 42 U.S.C. § 2000cc | Cruz v. Beto, 405 U.S. 319 (1972)

The First Amendment and the Religious Land Use and Institutionalized Persons Act (RLUIPA) protect your right to religious practice even inside a facility. You have the right to access religious texts — a Bible, Quran, Torah. You have the right to attend services when offered. You have the right to pray in your housing unit. Faith saved Keenan Hudson's life inside those walls. It was there that he found God and built the spiritual foundation of everything he has accomplished since. Your faith is yours. No one inside can legally take it from you.

SCENARIO — Jaylen, Age 15

Jaylen asked for a Bible three times in two weeks. Each time he was told there were none available. On his fourth request, a staff member told him religious materials were 'not a priority.'

What happened: Jaylen's family contacted the facility chaplain and cited RLUIPA. The chaplain escalated to administration. A Bible was delivered to Jaylen within 48 hours. The family documented the entire exchange in writing.

■ REMEMBER THIS: Under RLUIPA, facilities cannot substantially burden your religious practice. Religious texts are a right — not a privilege.

■ WHAT NOT TO DO

- **Don't accept 'unavailable' as an answer more than once — escalate to the chaplain in writing**

■ FOR PARENTS — What to do right now:

Contact the facility chaplain directly about your child's religious needs. A chaplain has specific authority over religious programming and materials. Put the request in writing so there is a record.

LAW #24

The Right to Access the Law Library

Bounds v. Smith, 430 U.S. 817 (1977) | Lewis v. Casey, 518 U.S. 343 (1996) | 37 Pa. Code § 93.12

The Supreme Court has held that incarcerated individuals have a constitutional right to meaningful access to the courts. This means access to legal materials, law library resources, and assistance preparing legal documents. If you are denied law library access, submit a written request each time and document the denial with the date and name of the staff member. Systematic denial of legal access is itself a constitutional violation that your lawyer can challenge.

SCENARIO — Marcus, Age 16

Marcus needed to review documents his lawyer sent and research his appeal. Staff denied him law library access four times over three weeks.

What happened: Marcus documented each denial with dates and staff names and passed the list to his mother. His lawyer filed a formal grievance citing Lewis v. Casey. Law library access was restored within two weeks and Marcus was given a designated weekly time slot.

■ **REMEMBER THIS: Every denial of legal access must be documented. Date, name, what was said. Give it to your family. This is your constitutional right.**

■ **WHAT NOT TO DO**

• **Don't accept repeated denials without documenting and reporting each one**

■ **FOR PARENTS — What to do right now:**

Ask your child whether they have been able to access the law library. If access is being blocked, raise it with the attorney immediately and in writing to the facility.

LAW #25

The Right to File Grievances Without Retaliation

1st Amendment, U.S. Constitution | 37 Pa. Code § 93.9 | PLRA — 42 U.S.C. § 1997e

You have the right to file a formal written grievance about how you are being treated. Staff are prohibited by law from retaliating against you for filing a grievance. Retaliation includes transfers to more restrictive units, loss of privileges, or increased scrutiny because you complained. File every grievance in writing. Ask for a grievance form by name. Submit it and ask for a receipt. Keep a copy — ask a family member to hold it if you cannot keep it safely. Your paper trail is the foundation of every legal challenge. Keenan Hudson learned inside those walls that the pen is mightier than the iron bar. Documentation is power.

SCENARIO — Bianca, Age 14

Bianca filed a detailed grievance about being denied medical care. Four days later she was transferred to a more restrictive unit. Staff called it a 'routine facility decision.' The timing told a different story.

What happened: Bianca's family documented the exact timeline — grievance filed, transfer date, gap between the two. Her lawyer sent a formal letter citing First Amendment retaliation case law. The facility was required to justify the transfer in writing. Their justification was thin. Bianca was returned to her original unit.

■ REMEMBER THIS: File every grievance. Document the date. Note any change in your treatment afterward. Retaliation is illegal and can be proven with a paper trail.

■ WHAT NOT TO DO

- **Don't file a grievance and fail to document what happens next — that follow-up record proves retaliation**
- **Don't assume nothing can be done about retaliation — it is actionable**

■ FOR PARENTS — What to do right now:

Ask your child at every visit: Have you filed any grievances? What happened after? Write down what they tell you with dates. If there is any sign of retaliation, report it to the lawyer immediately.

SPECIAL: CHARGE STACKING

What It Is, How It Works, and How to Fight It

Charge stacking is one of the most common and least understood tactics in the justice system. Understanding it is not optional — it is essential.

WHAT IS CHARGE STACKING?

Charge stacking is when a prosecutor files multiple separate criminal charges arising from a single incident. One physical altercation might result in charges of aggravated assault, simple assault, recklessly endangering another person, criminal conspiracy, terroristic threats, and possession of a weapon — all from the same 90-second event. Each charge carries its own potential sentence. When stacked, those sentences can theoretically add up to decades — creating enormous pressure to accept a plea deal, no matter how unfavorable.

WHY PROSECUTORS STACK CHARGES

Charge stacking is a deliberate strategy. When a defendant sees a list of 8, 10, or 12 charges, the psychological pressure to plead guilty to something — anything — becomes overwhelming. Prosecutors know this. Many cases resolve in plea deals not because the defendant is guilty of everything charged, but because the sheer number of charges makes fighting seem impossible. This is especially effective against young people and families who do not understand that charges can and must be challenged individually.

THE LAW: REMOVING CHARGES THAT DO NOT STICK

Every charge must be supported by evidence sufficient to prove each element of that specific offense beyond a reasonable doubt. If a charge lacks that foundation, the law provides specific tools:

• Motion for Nolle Prosequi (Pa. R. Crim. P. 561): The prosecution or defense asks the court to formally withdraw a charge that lacks sufficient evidence. When granted, that charge is dismissed from the case.

• Motion for Dismissal at Preliminary Hearing (Pa. R. Crim. P. 542): The defense argues the prosecution has not established a prima facie case for a specific charge. If the judge agrees, that charge is dismissed then and there.

• Motion in Limine: Before trial, the defense asks the judge to exclude evidence supporting certain charges. If the evidence is excluded, the charge it supported may fall with it.

• Post-Verdict Motions: If found not guilty on stacked charges at trial, those findings are permanent under double jeopardy protection.

KEY PRINCIPLE	A charge must be both legally valid AND supported by actual evidence. Your lawyer's job is to attack both — challenge whether the charge is legally supported AND whether there is real evidence. A charge with no evidence behind it should not survive a preliminary hearing.

WHAT YOU MUST DO

• Ask your lawyer to list every charge and identify which ones they plan to challenge and why.

• Ask specifically: 'Which of these charges does the prosecution have the weakest evidence for?'

• Ask whether any charges are duplicative — two charges that are basically the same thing described differently.

• Ask about filing a motion to dismiss unsupported charges at the preliminary hearing.

• Never accept a plea deal based on the total number of charges without understanding which ones could be knocked out through legal motions.

SCENARIO — Marcus, Age 16

Marcus was charged with seven offenses from one incident. His family was devastated and urged him to take the first plea deal just to get it over with. The deal offered two years of probation in exchange for guilty pleas on three charges — including one felony that would follow Marcus as an adult.

What happened: Marcus's lawyer asked for two weeks before responding. He filed motions challenging three of the seven charges. All three were dismissed for insufficient evidence. The prosecution, now with only four charges and a weaker case, came back with a significantly better offer — misdemeanor adjudication on two counts, no felony, clean record at 18. The difference was fighting the stack.

■ REMEMBER THIS: Never let the number of charges stop you from fighting. Each charge must be proven individually. A smaller, cleaner case often produces a far better outcome than accepting everything to make it stop.

SPECIAL: CERTIFICATION AS AN ADULT

The Full Story — What It Means and How to Fight It

Certification is the single most consequential legal event in a juvenile's case. It determines whether your child is treated as a child or an adult — and that difference can shape the next 30 to 40 years of their life.

THE TWO SYSTEMS SIDE BY SIDE

FACTOR	JUVENILE COURT → ADULT COURT
Name	Adjudication → Criminal Trial
Finding	Adjudicated Delinquent → Convicted of a Crime
System focus	Rehabilitation → Punishment
Record at 18	Can be sealed → Permanent public record
Employment	Minimal if sealed → Shows on every background check
Sentencing	Juvenile placement/probation → County jail or state prison
Court	Often closed to public → Open court, press attends

WHAT THE JUDGE CONSIDERS AT A CERTIFICATION HEARING (42 Pa. C.S. § 6355)

Age and maturity	Younger age and demonstrated immaturity weigh against certification

Juvenile system capacity	Can the juvenile system address this case effectively?
Prior record	First offense or a pattern of behavior?
Nature of the offense	How serious? Was it planned or impulsive?
Criminal sophistication	Opportunistic act or organized criminal behavior?
Rehabilitation potential	Can meaningful change happen before they age out of the system?
Public safety	Would keeping the case in juvenile court create safety concerns?
Community and family ties	School, family support, stable home environment

EVIDENCE THAT WINS CERTIFICATION HEARINGS

• School attendance records, grades, and any demonstrated improvement over time

• Letters from teachers, coaches, mentors, pastors, and community leaders — the more specific, the better

• Documentation of community involvement — sports, church, volunteer work, employment

• Mental health evaluation showing capacity for growth and rehabilitation

- Expert witness testimony on adolescent brain development and the science of youthful decision-making
- Family support documentation — stable home, parental supervision plan, family commitment
- Evidence of remorse and understanding of the harm caused
- Evidence that specific juvenile system programs can address this young person's needs

■ FOR PARENTS — What to do right now:

Start building the certification defense file the day your child is arrested. Do not wait until the hearing is scheduled. Gather school records, contact teachers and coaches, connect with a mental health professional. Every week of preparation matters enormously.

SPECIAL: THE FELONY MURDER RULE

What It Means — And the Fight for Change in Pennsylvania

This section exists because of the work Keenan Hudson is doing right now — inside SCI Phoenix, SCI Chester, and SCI Benner Township — with hundreds of people whose lives were changed forever by a law most people have never heard of.

WHAT IS THE FELONY MURDER RULE?

The felony murder rule holds that if a person is participating in a serious felony — such as robbery, burglary, or kidnapping — and someone is killed during that crime, every person involved can be charged with murder. Even if they did not commit the killing. Even if they did not know a killing would happen. Even if they did not have a weapon.

Being present and participating in a crime that results in a death — even accidentally, even against your knowledge — can result in a second-degree murder conviction with a mandatory life sentence.

KEENAN HUDSON'S STORY	At 15 years old, Keenan was part of a robbery. He did not fire the gun. He did not know the gun would be used. But someone died during that crime. Under the felony murder rule, Keenan was convicted of second-degree murder. He served nearly 15 years. His story is the story of hundreds across Pennsylvania — many incarcerated for 20, 30, 40, or even 50 years under this rule.

THE LEGAL FIGHT FOR CHANGE

Following U.S. Supreme Court decisions in Miller v. Alabama (2012) and Montgomery v. Louisiana (2016), which held that mandatory life without parole sentences for juveniles are unconstitutional, Pennsylvania courts have been reconsidering how mandatory life sentences for second-degree murder are applied to juvenile offenders. Cases connected to Commonwealth v. Derek Lee and related litigation have resulted in hundreds of individuals becoming newly eligible for resentencing hearings.

Over 400 individuals at SCI Phoenix alone — many incarcerated for decades — have become newly eligible. Keenan Hudson is on the ground inside these facilities every week, building trust, delivering books and curriculum, and helping people prepare for the possibility of coming home after 20, 30, 40, or even 50 years.

WHAT EVERY YOUNG PERSON MUST UNDERSTAND

- You can be convicted of murder even if you did not kill anyone — if a death occurred during a felony you were part of.

- Being present at a crime does not automatically make you equally culpable — but the law has historically treated it that way, and the fight to change that is ongoing.
- If you are charged with felony murder, your level of participation matters enormously — make sure your lawyer documents exactly what your role was.
- The Supreme Court has ruled that juveniles cannot receive mandatory life without parole — but you must assert this right through your attorney.
- If you or someone you know was convicted under the felony murder rule and may now be eligible for resentencing, contact The Re-Entry Connect Organization.

■ FOR PARENTS — What to do right now:

If your child is charged with a felony in which someone is injured or killed — even if your child had no weapon and did not intend for anyone to be hurt — get a lawyer immediately who understands the felony murder rule and how to challenge its application.

SPECIAL: EXPUNGEMENT & RECORD SEALING

The Path Forward — Life After the System

Your record does not have to follow you forever. Pennsylvania law provides real pathways to clean your record — but only if you know about them and take action. This section is about the future.

JUVENILE RECORD SEALING IN PENNSYLVANIA (Act 91 of 2018)

Under Pennsylvania's Act 91 of 2018, many juvenile records are now eligible for automatic sealing. If you were adjudicated delinquent for a non-violent offense and have no subsequent criminal record for a set period after your case closes, your juvenile record is sealed automatically. Once sealed, it cannot be seen by employers, landlords, or colleges. Some serious offenses — including most felony-level adjudications — are NOT eligible for automatic sealing.

EXPUNGEMENT — ERASING THE RECORD COMPLETELY

A juvenile can petition for expungement when: they have reached age 18, completed all terms of their juvenile disposition, have not been convicted of a felony in adult court, and five years have passed since the completion of all juvenile supervision. Courts look more favorably on expungement for lower-level adjudications.

ADULT RECORD — EXPUNGEMENT AND PARDON OPTIONS

• Summary Offense Expungement: If your adult conviction was for a summary offense, you may petition for expungement after 5 years with no subsequent arrests.

• Misdemeanor Expungement: Under PA Act 5 of 2016, certain misdemeanor convictions can be expunged after 10 years of clean record.

• Pardon from the Governor: For more serious convictions, a pardon can restore civil rights and potentially support expungement. The Board of Pardons reviews applications. This is a longer process but it is real.

• Clean Slate Act: Pennsylvania's Clean Slate Act (Act 56 of 2018) provides for automatic sealing of qualifying misdemeanor convictions after 10 years of no new arrests — without requiring a petition.

■ **KNOW THIS:**

Your record is not the end of your story. Keenan Hudson came home after nearly 15 years with a serious conviction and built businesses, purchased property, wrote bestselling books, earned a humanitarian award, and now serves as a commissioner for the City of Philadelphia. The path forward is real. It requires strategy, patience, and the right support. The Re-Entry Connect Organization exists to help you build that path.

■ FOR PARENTS — What to do right now:

As soon as your child's case is resolved and juvenile supervision is complete, talk to a lawyer about the expungement and sealing timeline. Mark the calendar. Do not let the eligibility window pass without taking action. A clean record is one of the most valuable assets your child can have building their future.

QUICK REFERENCE

The Exact Words to Use in Every Situation

When you are scared and your mind goes blank, these are the words that protect you. Practice them until they are automatic.

Police stop you	**'Am I being detained, or am I free to go?'**
You are detained	**'I am exercising my right to remain silent.'**
They ask to search	**'I do not consent to this search.'**
You are arrested	**'I want a lawyer. I am not answering any questions.'**
Questioned without parent	**'I want my parent and I want a lawyer before I answer anything.'**
Miranda not read	**Tell your lawyer: 'Nobody read me my rights before they questioned me.'**
In court — confused	**Tell your lawyer: 'Explain every charge before I agree to anything.'**
Denied medical care	**'I am submitting a sick call request in writing right now.'**

Denied law library	**'I am formally requesting law library access in writing.'**
Mistreated inside	**'I need a grievance form. I am filing a formal written grievance.'**
Phone call from jail	**'I've been arrested. I'm at [location]. Get me a lawyer.' Nothing else.**
About charge stacking	**Ask your lawyer: 'Which of these charges can we challenge for lack of evidence?'**

PENNSYLVANIA LEGAL RESOURCES

Organizations That Can Help

If you are inside a facility, give this page to a parent, counselor, or trusted adult outside and ask them to make contact on your behalf.

Defender Association of Philadelphia

Juvenile Unit: (215) 568-3190

1441 Sansom Street, Philadelphia, PA 19102

Free public defense for those who cannot afford a lawyer — Philadelphia

---

Juvenile Law Center

(215) 625-0551

1315 Walnut Street, Suite 400, Philadelphia, PA 19107

Nonprofit advocacy and legal representation for children in the justice system

---

Support Center for Child Advocates

(215) 387-5955

1617 JFK Blvd, Suite 1200, Philadelphia, PA 19103

Legal and social services for vulnerable children

Pennsylvania Innocence Project

(717) 728-3640

Widener University, Harrisburg, PA

For those who believe they were wrongfully convicted

PA Board of Pardons

(717) 787-2596

333 Market Street, Harrisburg, PA 17126

For pardon applications on adult criminal convictions

The Re-Entry Connect Organization

thereentryconnect@gmail.com

PO Box 95, 521 Central Ave, Cheltenham, PA 19012

Reentry support, resources, books, curriculum, and advocacy — www.thereentryconnect.org

---

10 QUESTIONS TO ASK YOUR LAWYER ON DAY ONE

- What are all the charges against me and what does each one mean?
- Is the prosecution seeking to certify me as an adult?
- What is the specific evidence for each charge?
- Which charges do you plan to challenge and how?
- Were my Miranda rights read before I was questioned?
- Was there a valid probable cause basis for my arrest?
- What happens at the preliminary hearing and should I waive it?
- What does each plea offer mean — what am I admitting to and what follows me?

- What is the realistic range of outcomes if we fight versus take a deal?
- Can my record be sealed or expunged after this case is resolved?

GLOSSARY

40+ Words You Need to Know

Adjudication	The juvenile court equivalent of a trial.
Arraignment	First court appearance after arrest. Charges read and plea entered.
Bail	Money or conditions set by a judge to allow release before trial.
Certification	Legal process of moving a juvenile case to adult criminal court.
Clean Slate Act	PA law that automatically seals qualifying misdemeanor convictions after 10 years.
Concurrent Sentences	Sentences served at the same time — you serve only the longest one.
Consecutive Sentences	Sentences served one after another — total time adds up.
Confrontation Clause	Your 6th Amendment right to face and cross-examine witnesses against you.

Decertification	Successful fight to move a case from adult court back to juvenile court.
Delinquent	A juvenile court finding that a young person committed an offense.
Detained	Legally held by police. Must stay but do not have to answer questions.
Disposition	Juvenile court equivalent of a sentence.
Double Jeopardy	Constitutional protection against being tried twice for the same crime after a not-guilty verdict.
Due Process	Your right to fair treatment under the law at every stage.
Expungement	Legal destruction of a criminal or juvenile record.
Felony Murder Rule	Doctrine holding all participants in a felony responsible for any death that occurs.
Grievance	A formal written complaint filed inside a facility about treatment or conditions.
IEP	Individualized Education Program — a federal legal plan for students with special learning needs.

Invoke	To formally assert a legal right.
JJDPA	Juvenile Justice and Delinquency Prevention Act — requires sight and sound separation of juveniles from adults.
Mandatory Minimum	A minimum sentence required by law that a judge cannot go below.
Miranda Rights	Rights read to suspects before custodial questioning.
Miranda Violation	Police question someone in custody without reading Miranda rights — statements may be suppressed.
Motion	A formal legal request to a judge asking for a specific ruling or action.
Motion for Nolle Prosequi	Motion to formally withdraw and dismiss a specific charge.
Multiplicity	Filing multiple charges that are essentially the same offense — a form of charge stacking.
Pardon	Formal forgiveness of a criminal conviction granted by the Governor.
Plea Deal	Agreement where a defendant pleads guilty to reduced charges for a lighter sentence.

Plead the Fifth	Exercising your 5th Amendment right not to testify against yourself.
Preliminary Hearing	Hearing to determine if enough evidence exists to send a case to trial.
Prima Facie	Latin for 'on its face' — enough evidence to move a case forward to trial.
Probable Cause	Specific articulable facts giving police reason to believe a crime occurred.
Probation	Supervised release program as an alternative to incarceration.
Record Sealing	Making a juvenile or criminal record invisible to the public.
RLUIPA	Federal protection of religious practice in facilities.
Sight and Sound Separation	Federal requirement that juveniles cannot be housed where they can see or hear adults.
Stacked Charges	Multiple charges filed from a single incident to maximize legal pressure.
Suppress / Suppression	Judge ruling that evidence or statements cannot be used because obtained illegally.

Waive	To give up a legal right. NEVER waive a right without fully understanding what you are giving up.
Zero Bond	Being held with no possibility of bail — typically for homicide or very serious charges.

MY NOTES — WHAT HAPPENED

Write down everything. Date. Time. Names. What was said. What was done. This paper is your protection.

MY NOTES — COURT DATES & HEARINGS

Write down every hearing date, what was decided, what your lawyer said, what the judge said.

MY NOTES — NAMES & CONTACTS

Write down every officer name, lawyer name, judge name, case number, and any contact information you receive.

MY NOTES — GRIEVANCES FILED

Every grievance you file: write the date, what it was about, who you gave it to, and what response you received.

MY NOTES — CONTINUED

Use this page for anything else that matters. Documentation is power.

A FINAL WORD

From Keenan Hudson

You made it to the end of this booklet. That means something.

It means you are taking your situation seriously. It means you understand that knowledge is not optional — it is survival. It means you are choosing to fight with your mind instead of just with your circumstances.

I want you to know something that took me years to fully understand: the system is not all-powerful. It has rules. And when you know those rules better than the people enforcing them, the balance of power shifts. Not all the way — not overnight. But it shifts. And sometimes that shift is the difference between your future and the absence of one.

I was 15 years old sitting in a cell with a Bible my grandmother told me to take. I didn't fully understand why she insisted. I do now. She wasn't just giving me comfort. She was reminding me that I had something inside me that could not be locked up. That no sentence, no charge, no courtroom, and no wall could touch what I chose to build on the inside.

You have that same thing. Use this booklet. Use your rights. Use your mind. And when you come out the other side — and you will — use your story to help the next person who needs it. That is how cycles break. That is how communities heal. That is how we change the story.

Write to us. Let us know how you are doing. We mean that.

With everything I have —

Keenan Hudson

Keenan Hudson Enterprise LLC | DBA The Re-Entry Connect Solutions

PO Box 95, 521 Central Ave, Cheltenham, PA 19012

www.thereentryconnect.org | www.keenanhudson.com

BONUS CHAPTER — CHAPTER 26

HOW TO FILE A LAWSUIT

County · State · Federal

When Your Rights Are Violated — Here Is What You Do

What This Chapter Is About

You have rights. We spent 25 chapters teaching you what those rights are. But what happens when someone inside a facility — a guard, a staff member, a warden — violates those rights anyway? What do you do? Who do you tell?

This chapter gives you the answer step by step. It covers the grievance process first — because by law you must try to fix the problem inside the facility before going to court. Then it covers how to file a lawsuit, who to contact, and what the chain of command looks like at the county, state, and federal level.

■ IMPORTANT — READ THIS FIRST

Before you can sue in court, you must go through the grievance process inside the facility first. If you skip this step, the judge will throw your case out. This is required by the Prison Litigation Reform Act (PLRA), 42 U.S.C. § 1997e(a). It applies to everyone — state prison, county jail, and juvenile detention.

PART 1: THE CHAIN OF COMMAND

Every facility has a chain of command. You must start at the bottom and work up. If you skip someone, your grievance can be thrown out. Here is the chain for Pennsylvania state prisons:

Tell them about the problem first. If nothing changes within a reasonable time, move to Level 2 and file a written grievance.

File your DC-804 Inmate Grievance Form with this person. They handle all official written grievances inside the facility.

If the Grievance Officer denies your grievance, appeal to the Facility Manager. They are the top officer of the prison.

Final internal appeal in the PA DOC system. Once SOIGA responds — or fails to respond on time — you have exhausted your remedies and may file in court.

For urgent matters, write directly to the DOC Secretary at: 1920 Technology Pkwy, Mechanicsburg, PA 17050 | ra-crpadocsecretary@pa.gov

Only after exhausting all internal steps above can you file a Section 1983 lawsuit in U.S. District Court.

PART 2: THE GRIEVANCE PROCESS — STEP BY STEP

Pennsylvania state prisons use DC-ADM 804. Every step has a deadline. Missing a deadline can end your case. Follow these steps exactly and keep copies of everything.

Write down exactly what happened before you file anything. Date, time, location, officer name or badge number, what they did, what you said, who saw it. Be specific. Keep your notes safe and ask someone outside to hold a copy.

Ask your counselor or housing officer for a DC-804 Inmate Grievance Form. If they refuse, write down that refusal with the date and name. You must file this form within 15 working days of the incident. Do not wait.

Describe what happened, state which right was violated, and state exactly what you want. CRITICAL: If you want money damages, write that on this first form. You cannot add money damages later. Sign, date it, and keep a copy before submitting.

Submit the form and ask for written confirmation. The Grievance Officer must respond within 15 working days. If they do not respond in time, you can still appeal to the next level.

If denied, you have 15 working days to appeal to the Facility Manager using DC-804 Part 2. Explain why the response was wrong. Keep a copy of everything.

If the Facility Manager denies your appeal, file a final appeal with SOIGA using DC-804 Part 3. You have 15 working days. When SOIGA issues a final decision — or fails to respond on time — you have exhausted all remedies and may file in federal court.

■ EXHAUSTION COMPLETE

When SOIGA issues its final decision (or fails to respond on time), write down the date. Save every piece of paper from every step. You will need all of it in court.

GRIEVANCE DEADLINES AT A GLANCE

Step	Who Acts	Deadline
File grievance	You → Grievance Officer	15 working days from incident
Response	Grievance Officer → You	15 working days
1st Appeal	You → Facility Manager	15 working days after denial
Final Appeal	You → SOIGA	15 working days after Mgr denial
File lawsuit	You → Federal Court	After SOIGA final decision

PART 3: WHICH COURT DO YOU FILE IN?

The court you file in depends on WHERE you are being held. A state prison, a county jail, and a juvenile detention center are three completely different systems with different rules. Read the section below that matches your situation.

Where You Are Held	Where to File — Law Used
STATE PRISON (SCI Phoenix, SCI Chester, SCI Benner, etc.)	U.S. District Court (Federal) 42 U.S.C. § 1983
COUNTY JAIL (Philadelphia, Delaware Co., Montgomery Co., etc.)	U.S. District Court (Federal) 42 U.S.C. § 1983
JUVENILE DETENTION (Philadelphia JJC, YDC, county detention)	U.S. District Court (Federal) 42 U.S.C. § 1983 AND/OR PA Court of Common Pleas — Family Division
FEDERAL PRISON (Federal BOP facility)	U.S. District Court (Federal) Bivens Action
STATE LAW VIOLATIONS (some cases)	PA Court of Common Pleas Pennsylvania state law

IF YOU ARE IN A COUNTY JAIL

County jails are run by the county — not the state. You do NOT use the PA DOC grievance system (DC-ADM 804). Every county jail has its own grievance procedure.

1. Ask your housing officer for the facility's inmate grievance form and ask to see the written grievance policy.
2. File your grievance with the Grievance Officer or Jail Administrator in writing. Keep a copy of everything.
3. If denied, appeal to the Warden or Jail Administrator.
4. If denied again, appeal to the County Director of Corrections or County Board of Commissioners.
5. Once all internal steps are complete, you have exhausted your remedies and may file a Section 1983 lawsuit in U.S. District Court.

KEY CONTACTS — COUNTY JAILS

Philadelphia Prison System (PPS)
(215) 685-8200
1451 State Road, Philadelphia, PA 19136

Philadelphia Inspector General
(215) 686-1770
One Parkway Building, Philadelphia, PA 19102

Delaware County Prison
(610) 891-4729
500 Cheyney Road, Thornton, PA 19373

Montgomery County Correctional Facility
(610) 278-3900
60 Eagleville Road, Eagleville, PA 19408

Bucks County Correctional Facility

(215) 773-6600

1730 S. Easton Road, Doylestown, PA 18901

Chester County Prison

(610) 344-6930

501 Bond Avenue, Coatesville, PA 19320

IF YOU ARE IN A JUVENILE DETENTION CENTER

Juvenile detention centers are run by the county Department of Human Services (DHS) — not the PA DOC. Your path to court is different, and in some cases faster, because your attorney can file motions in Juvenile Court directly.

1. Tell your counselor or Juvenile Probation Officer (JPO) what happened right away. Ask for a grievance form. Write down everything with dates and names.
2. File a formal written complaint with the Facility Superintendent or Program Director. Keep a copy.
3. If unresolved, escalate in writing to the County DHS Director or the County Juvenile Justice Director.
4. Contact your juvenile court attorney or public defender immediately. They can file a motion in PA Court of Common Pleas — Family Division to address unsafe conditions. This is often the fastest path to relief.
5. For serious constitutional violations, file a Section 1983 lawsuit in U.S. District Court after exhausting internal steps.
6. Contact the Juvenile Law Center or PA Child Advocate immediately. They can sometimes intervene faster than a court filing.

KEY CONTACTS — JUVENILE DETENTION

Philadelphia Juvenile Justice Services Center (JJC)
(215) 686-5400
8801 Penrose Avenue, Philadelphia, PA 19153

Philadelphia Dept. of Human Services (DHS)

(215) 683-6000

1515 Arch Street, Philadelphia, PA 19102

PA Juvenile Court Judges Commission

(717) 795-2000

PO Box 60457, Harrisburg, PA 17106

Juvenile Law Center

(215) 625-0551

1315 Walnut Street, Suite 400, Philadelphia, PA 19107 | www.jlc.org

---

PA Child Advocate — Governor's Office

(800) 692-7286

333 Market Street, 12th Floor, Harrisburg, PA 17126

PA DHS Inspector General

(800) 932-0582

Pennsylvania DHS, Harrisburg, PA 17105 | Abuse complaints

PART 4: HOW TO FILE YOUR CIVIL RIGHTS LAWSUIT

Now that you have exhausted your grievances, you can take your case to court. The main law you will use is Section 1983 — 42 U.S.C. § 1983. This lets you sue any government official who violated your constitutional rights while doing their job.

You need every grievance form you filed, every response you received, your notes, witness names, dates, and any medical records if you were injured. Do not go to court without all of this documentation.

A pro se form lets you file yourself without a lawyer. Every federal district court has a free form for prisoners. Write to the Clerk of Court at the nearest federal courthouse and ask for the 'Pro Se Prisoner Civil Rights Complaint Form.' They will mail it at no cost.

State: (1) Your name and prisoner number. (2) The name of every person who violated your rights. (3) Exactly what they did and when. (4) Which constitutional rights were violated. (5) What you want the court to do. Be specific. Judges dismiss vague cases.

The federal court filing fee is $405 as of 2026. If you cannot afford it, file an In Forma Pauperis (IFP) form asking the court to let you pay in installments from your commissary account. Mail the original complaint and one copy to the Clerk of the District Court where the violation happened.

If a court dismisses three of your lawsuits as frivolous, you receive a strike. After three strikes, you cannot file for free unless you are in immediate danger of serious physical injury. Only file cases you honestly believe are strong.

After filing, the judge reviews your complaint. This is called screening. Weak cases may be dismissed here. If your case passes, the court orders defendants to respond. This can take several months. Keep copies of everything.

Filing a lawsuit is hard. If you can get a lawyer, get one. Many civil rights attorneys take prison cases on contingency — paid only if you win. Contact the organizations in Part 5. If your case is strong and remedies are exhausted, an attorney will often help at no cost.

PART 5: WHO TO CONTACT — THE FULL DIRECTORY

Give this list to a family member outside. If you are inside a facility, pass this page to your family and ask them to make contact on your behalf.

PENNSYLVANIA DOC — INTERNAL CHAIN

PA DOC Central Office
(717) 728-2573
1920 Technology Pkwy, Mechanicsburg, PA 17050 | ra-contactdoc@pa.gov

DOC Secretary's Office
ra-crpadocsecretary@pa.gov
1920 Technology Pkwy, Mechanicsburg, PA 17050

SOIGA — Final Grievance Appeals
(717) 728-2573
1920 Technology Pkwy, Mechanicsburg, PA 17050 | DC-804 Part 3 final appeals

SCI Phoenix
(610) 495-6520
1200 Mokychic Drive, Collegeville, PA 19426

SCI Chester
(610) 490-4100
500 E. 4th Street, Chester, PA 19013

SCI Benner Township
(814) 355-4874
301 Institution Drive, Bellefonte, PA 16823

FEDERAL DISTRICT COURTS — PENNSYLVANIA

Eastern District of PA — Philadelphia Area
(215) 597-7704
601 Market Street, Philadelphia, PA 19106 | For SCI Chester, SCI Phoenix, Philadelphia facilities

Middle District of PA — Central PA

(570) 348-2800 or (717) 221-4482

235 N. Washington Ave, Scranton | 1501 N. 6th St, Harrisburg | For SCI Benner Township

Western District of PA — Pittsburgh Area

(412) 208-7500

700 Grant Street, Pittsburgh, PA 15219

CIVIL RIGHTS & LEGAL AID ORGANIZATIONS

Juvenile Law Center

(215) 625-0551

1315 Walnut Street, Suite 400, Philadelphia, PA 19107 | www.jlc.org

ACLU of Pennsylvania

(215) 923-4357

PO Box 60173, Philadelphia, PA 19102 | www.aclupa.org

Defender Association of Philadelphia

(215) 568-3190

1441 Sansom Street, Philadelphia, PA 19102 | Juvenile Unit

PA Legal Aid Network

(717) 236-9486

www.palawhelp.org | Free civil legal help statewide

PA Innocence Project

(717) 728-3640

Widener University, Harrisburg, PA

National ACLU — National Prison Project

(212) 549-2500

125 Broad Street, New York, NY 10004

The Re-Entry Connect Organization

thereentryconnect@gmail.com

PO Box 95, 521 Central Ave, Cheltenham, PA 19012 | www.thereentryconnect.org

OVERSIGHT & COMPLAINT OFFICES

PA DOJ — Civil Rights Division

(215) 861-8200

615 Chestnut Street, Suite 1250, Philadelphia, PA 19106

U.S. DOJ Civil Rights — Special Litigation

(202) 514-6255

950 Pennsylvania Ave NW, Washington, DC 20530

Middle District U.S. Attorney

(717) 221-4482

1501 N. 6th Street, Harrisburg, PA 17102 | usapam.contact@usdoj.gov

PA Office of Inspector General

(800) 932-0936

555 Walnut Street, Harrisburg, PA 17101

PA Governor's Office

(717) 787-2500

508 Main Capitol Building, Harrisburg, PA 17120 | ra-govinfo@pa.gov

PART 6: WHAT YOU CAN WIN IN COURT

If your lawsuit is successful, here is what a court can give you:

Money Damages — Compensatory

Money for your injury, pain, medical bills, or other real harm caused by the violation of your rights.

Money Damages — Punitive

Extra money to punish a defendant who acted in an especially bad or intentional way. This is on top of compensatory damages.

Injunction

A court order telling the facility to stop doing something — stop putting juveniles in solitary, provide proper medical care, or stop retaliating against you.

Declaratory Relief

A court statement that your rights were violated. Creates an official legal record and supports future claims.

■ IMPORTANT LIMIT

Under the PLRA, you cannot sue for emotional harm alone. You must show a real physical injury to receive money damages for pain and suffering. Document every physical injury with medical records and written reports.

PART 7: YOUR QUICK CHECKLIST

Use this checklist every time your rights are violated. Work through it from top to bottom.

- Write down what happened — date, time, location, officer name, exactly what they did
- Get a DC-804 Grievance Form (state prison) or your facility's grievance form (county jail or juvenile detention)
- Fill out the form — describe what happened, which right was violated, what you want
- Write 'money damages' on the FIRST form if you want to be paid for your injury
- Submit within 15 working days of the incident
- Keep a copy of everything you submit
- Get written confirmation that the form was received
- Wait for the response — 15 working days
- If denied, appeal to the Facility Manager within 15 working days
- If denied again, appeal to SOIGA (state) or County Director (county jail) within 15 working days
- When SOIGA or the final level responds (or fails to respond on time) — remedies are exhausted
- Contact a civil rights lawyer or legal aid organization right away
- Request a Pro Se Complaint Form from the Clerk of the federal District Court
- Fill out the Section 1983 complaint with all documentation attached

- File an In Forma Pauperis (IFP) form if you cannot afford the $405 filing fee
- Keep copies of absolutely everything you file — forever

A Final Word

I know this process looks long and complicated. It is. The system was not designed to make it easy for you to fight back. That is intentional. But people do fight back. People win.

I watched men and women inside SCI Phoenix, SCI Chester, and SCI Benner Township file grievances, exhaust their remedies, and take their cases to federal court. Some of them won. Some changed policies for everyone who came after them.

The pen is mightier than the iron bar. Documentation is power. Exhaust your remedies. Keep every piece of paper. And if you need help, write to us.

Keenan Hudson

Founder, The Re-Entry Connect Organization

PO Box 95, 521 Central Ave, Cheltenham, PA 19012

www.thereentryconnect.org | thereentryconnect@gmail.com

YOU ARE NOT ALONE.

You have rights. Use them.

"Success is obtained by utilizing the right strategies."

— Keenan Hudson

REACH OUT TO US

Keenan Hudson Enterprise LLC

DBA The Re-Entry Connect Solutions

Write to us:

PO Box 95, 521 Central Ave

Cheltenham, PA 19012

Give this address to a parent, counselor, or trusted adult outside

IF YOU ARE INSIDE A FACILITY:

Give this book to a parent or trusted adult.

Ask them to contact us on your behalf.

www.thereentryconnect.org | www.keenanhudson.com

ISBN: 979-8-9964989-2-5